The Elements in Poetry

WATER

Published in 2007 by Evans Brothers Limited
2A Portman Mansions
Chiltern St
London W1U 6NR

British Library Cataloguing in Publication Data
Water. - (The elements of poetry)
    1. Water - Juvenile poetry
    I. Peters, Andrew (Andrew Fusek)
    808.8'1936

    ISBN-10: 023752886X
13-digit ISBN 9780237528867

Editorial: Julia Bird & Su Swallow
Design: Simon Borrough
Production: Jenny Mulvanny

Contents

Voices of Water

The water in the rain says **Tick Tick Tack**
The water in the sleet says Slush
The water in the ice says **Crick Crick Crack**
The water in the snow says Hush

The water in the sink says Slosh Slosh
The water in the tap says Drip
The water in the bath says Wash Wash
The water in the cup says Sip

The water in the pool says Splish Splash
The water in the stream says **Trill**
The water in the sea says **Crish Crash**
The water in the pond... stays still.

The water in the soil says Sow, Sow
The water in the cloud says Give
The water in the plant says Grow, Grow
The water in the world says Live

Tony Mitton

To Solve a Drought

Bird, the boy said,
pierce the skin of the cloud above
the dark grey cloud.

Or better still, bird, unzipper
the cloud, let the inside rain
tumble out.

But if you can't pierce or unzip,
try peeling it like an orange
and let the juicy rain dribble out.

I'll have my mouth open
and so will this paddock.
Bird, next year's grass seeds and insects
depend on your efforts,
so fly to it
now.

Lorraine Marwood

The River

Little-trickler, Moss-tickler, Snow-swallower, Slope-follower, Hill-tumbler,

Falling-thunderer, Valley-maker, Plain-snaker, Soft-gurgler,

Soil-burglar, Thirst-quencher, Splashing-drencher, Rain-gulper, Tree-pulper,

Flood-bringer, Mud-slinger, Sea-feeder, Cloud-breeder: Reborn as rain, Begin again...

Kevin McCann

Nine Mice

Nine mice on tiny tricycles
went riding on the ice,
they rode in spite of warning signs,
they rode despite advice.

The signs were right, the ice was thin,
in half a trice, the mice fell in,
and from their chins down to their toes,
those mice entirely froze.

Nine mindless mice, who paid the price,
are thawing slowly by the ice,
still sitting on their tricycles
...nine white and shiny micicles!

Jack Prelutsky

Pull the other one!

'H_2O... that's water,'
Claimed our teacher, Mrs Pugh -
So I peered down a microscope
To see if it were true.

The drop I saw had bubbles
But tell me please won't you...
Why I couldn't find one H
Or single tiny 2!

Philip Waddell

Rodney Reid

In his bathtub Rodney Reid is
Making quite a mess,
This disproving Archimedes'
Principle, no less.

{Note the body in this case is
but a boy of four,
Yet the fluid it displaces
Covers all the floor.}

Colin West

Note - Archimedes' Principle: When a body is immersed in water, its apparent loss of weight is equal to the weight of water displaced.

10

Water Project

Teacher's voice,
Quite firm:

"Water project
This term.

Huge subject,
Vast scope ...
Fascinating!"

We hope.

"Think wet ...
Tell you what:
Walk in rain!"
Thanks a lot.

Water closets,
Water clocks,
Pipes, cisterns,
Stopcocks.

Water towers,
Water wheels;
Perch, dace,
Pike, eels.

Dip pond:
All smelly.
Green slime
Fills welly.

Water birds:
Duck, swan.
Water project
Drags on.

Water boatmen,
Water fleas,
Lakes, pools,
Springs, seas.

Water music
(That's Handel's),
Water beds,
Water candles.

Waterfalls:
It does.
Water torture
It was.

Eric Finney

Ice

Was the first time
Anyone remembers it happening

The fields froze
In our village
In South China

We broke some
Not knowing what it was
And took it to the junk peddler

He thought it was glass
And traded us a penny for it

He wrapped it up
In an old cloth and placed it
On top of his basket

Of course
The noon day sun melted it

By the time
We came back with more
He had gotten wise

Jim Wong-Chu

Weathers

This is the weather the cuckoo likes,
And so do I;
When showers betumble the chestnut spikes,
And nestlings fly;
And the little brown nightingale bills his best,
And they sit outside at 'The Traveller's Rest',
And maids come forth sprig-muslin drest,
And citizens dream of the south and the west,
And so do I.

This is the weather the shepherd shuns,
And so do I;
When beeches drip in brown and duns,
And thresh, and ply;
And hill-hid tides throb, throe on throe,
And meadow rivulets overflow,
And drops on gate-bars hang in a row,
And rooks in families homeward go,
And so do I.

Thomas Hardy

Fog

The fog comes
on little cat feet.

It sits looking
over harbor and city
on silent haunches
and then moves on.

Carl Sandburg

Water cycle

Evaporation
Condensation
Precipitation

Letting off steam
Cooling down
Tears of regret

Mike Jubb

Water-Cycle

Hot sun soak her up,
Cold cloud spit her out,
With a shout of thunder
How she falls.
Falls asleep, lies deep.
Mountains weep and dream
And in the dream she seems to grow,
Stronger, longer,
Full of river-longing
Wide awake, thrills like a milkshake shivers,
She spills into the land.
But then a man made hand stop her dead
With a dam.
Down, down, down underground, rushing round,
Pushed around by endless fists of metal how she weeps.
Someone twists the tap.
Tap, kettle, cup of tea, into me and out of me.
Down the drain, underground, rushing round
Spilling into land
And filling out the sea where the hot sun waits
How she sings!

Andrew Fusek Peters

Snagger's Pond

Snagger's Pond was dying.
There was bad pollution.
So, what could we do?
What *was* the solution?

We dragged out bicycle tyres,
Rusty wheels, soggy plastic bags,
An old brolly, worn trainers,
Tangled twine and rotting rags.
We pulled out a Wellington boot,
A headless doll, slimy stones,
Handfuls of decaying leaves,
Bats and balls, beanbags and bones.

Then we hosed in water for hours,
Introduced scores of water snails,
Aquatic plants, green duckweed,
Frogspawn, and pebbles in pails.
We put in a pair of newts,
And fish - a dozen or more -
Then watched the minnows, ghost carp,
And small shubunkins explore.

Snagger's pond was dying.
There was bad pollution.
So, we cleaned and restocked.
We *found* the solution.

Graveyard Scene

There are no names on the gravestone now.
They've been washed away by the rain.
The graveyard trees are skeletons now,
They will never wear leaves again.

Instead of a forest, the tower surveys
A bleak and desolate plain.
Those are not tears in the gargoyle's eyes,
They are droplets of acid rain.

John Foster

# Man, the Mad Magician

Said the money-man "We must have oil!
And that's my final word!"
How magical and tragical his final act
As the seagull became a blackbird.

Andrew Fusek Peters

Washing the Sky

I start with the windows;
Their stale breath of winter grimes
Glass, blinks out sun.

Next I sluice floors,
Tip away brown bubbles of sludge,
Take a stiff brush, swab

The yard; moss releases
Its green grip, flags gleam redly
Under suds. Then I wash

Each blade of grass,
Every bud and daffodil; they dry
Jewel bright. The great sail cloth

Sky is last; I shake the pillowcase
Clouds, snap and slap at creases,
A whirlwind whipping; I peg

Them out; great billows
Puff up, sweet-talking wind socks
Gust nine to the dozen, lace

White hope with silver. I laugh
In the wild wide freedom, stretch
And turn the year towards summer.

Margaret Gleave

19

Girl, 13, Malawi

Sun rises, so do we:
Three brothers, father, me.

I'm mother now, must take
Our two zinc buckets
Twenty minutes' walk to where
The milk-grey liquid lies.
It wears a cloth of
floating green and brown
That I must part
To dip beneath, try not to look
At all the things that wriggle there.
Skim off the browny froth
And carry carefully
The buckets, full, twenty minutes back.
I try to boil it, but look:
Few trees; there's very little wood for fire.
And when I do
It stinks and makes a foam on top.
My smallest brother cries. He's sick.
The water makes his tummy ill,
But still, he needs to drink.
We cook. We wash. Two buckets empty.
So, twenty minutes walk again,
Twenty back.
Look after brothers. Make our tiny meal.
Little brother very hot,
But also very quiet.
So I can slip away again
To walk and dip and carry.

What to do as the sun slips low?
Dream clean water will one day flow.

Girl, 13, UK

"Wakey wakey sleepy head!"
9.00am fall out of bed,
stumble off into the shower
"Will I be long? No. Just an hour."
Wash my hair, condition too,
Clean teeth {3 minutes}, flush the loo,
Antibacterial face-wash gel
Scrub-a-dub and rinse it well.
Blow nose as heading to the door,
Tissue in loo and flush once more.
Off to the kitchen, kettle on
But fridge door empty! Milk all gone!
Make do with glass of squash instead
Take drink and toast back up to bed.
Saturday: my day for chores:
Wash the car and mop the floors;
Water lawn and keep it green;
Put several loads in the washing machine.
Jobs done: pocket money time.
Hand it over! Mine, all mine!
I'll spend it all on something cool
Then head off to the swimming pool.
Splash, splash, splash! Then time for home
Rinse chlorine off with shower foam.

What to do with the evening ahead?
Relaxing bath, then time for bed.

Polly Peters

Statistics:

1 in 5 people in the world live without access to clean water

Half the people in the world have no sanitation {toilet and washing facilities}

Every 15 seconds, a child dies from a water-related disease

Unsafe drinking water is the world's number one killer

Low Tide at Night

Mounds of seaweed whisper.
Salt seeps into the sand.
Limpets browse, scrape tracks along boulders
Etching grey scrolls into dark algae.

Lugworms hide in mud caves
Marked by coils and holes
That open and close in measured time;
Seven gulps of air till the flood tide.

Circled by bladder-wrack
Rock pools are black opals.
Pebbles and shells discarded by waves
Freckle a beach bare of daytime hordes.

Far off, asleep, the sea:
Lights mark another shore.
Meantime, a crab waits his hardening shell
Under a blanket of whispered seaweed song.

Catherine Benson

From Paradise Lost

There Leviathan,
Hugest of all living creatures,
in the deep
Stretched like a promontory
sleeps or swims,
And seems a moving land;
and at his gills
Draws in, and at his breath
spouts out a sea.

John Milton

seashell

They've brought me a seashell.

Inside it sings
A map of the sea.
My heart
Fills up with water,
With smallish fish
Of shade and silver.

They've brought me a seashell.

Federico Garcia Lorca

The Fishermen's Song

O blithely shines the bonnie sun
Upon the Isle of May,
And blithely rolls the morning tide
Into St Andrew's bay.

When haddocks leave the Firth of Forth
And mussels leave the shore,
When oysters climb up Berwick Law
We'll go to sea no more,
No more,
We'll go to sea no more.

Anon

The Tempest, Act 1, Scene 2

Miranda:

If by your art, my dearest father, you have
Put the wild waters in this roar, allay them.
The sky, it seems would pour down stinking pitch,
But that the sea, mounting to a welkin's* cheek
Dashes the fire out. O I have suffer'd
With those that I saw suffer! A brave vessel,
Who had no doubt some noble creatures in her,
Dashed all to pieces. O the cry did knock
Against my very heart! Pour souls! They perish'd.
Had I been any god of power, I would
Have sunk the sea within the earth, or e'er
It should the good ship so have swallow'd, and
The freighting souls within her.

William Shakespeare

* a *welkin* is an archaic word for sky or 'the vault of heaven', 'the bowl of the sky'

Puddle

The moon, the stars, the clouds, a plane
And all that my sky can contain
Reflected in a pool of rain.

This is the eye that follows the sky.

A sheet lain on the bare terrain
That's picture-smooth and mirror-plain
Like looking through a window-pane.

This is the mouth that swallows the sky.

Brilliant echo, bright refrain
Each tiny detail you retain
Write it down and tell it again.

This is the hand that borrows the sky.

Reflected in a pool of rain
My sky with what it can contain:
A bird, the sun, a plane again.

Nick Toczek

Rain in the City

I had only known the splash
and the pelt and the scatter,
the gush and the gurgle of gutters
and the tumbled drums of the thunder –
until I looked downwards from an upstairs
office-block
and saw the sudden flowering
of a thousand umbrellas
in a most unlikely spring.

Anne Bell

Flood

The rain fell all night, beating on roofs
As dark and hunched as hills,
Cascading uncontained into the street
In wind-curved waterfalls.

All night the rain fell, kept falling.
This morning, the street's a river;
Cars founder and sink, while buses
Crawl laden as ocean liners,

Raise bow-waves so swollen they break
Booming across the pavement
Where tossed at the tide's rising mark
Seaweed tangles to litter;

And under hedges and gates
Fish shoal in the gleaming shallows,
And further out, through the channel
Marked by wave-slapped traffic-lights,

Dolphins leap lampposts, and whales
Surge and sound in the deep roads.

Dave Calder

Author index

Acknowledgements

Catherine Benson: 'Low Tide at Night', by permission of the author.

Dave Calder: © Dave Calder 2002 (from **Dolphins Leap Lamposts**, Macmillan), by permission of the author.

Jim Wong-Chu: 'Ice', reprinted with permission from **Chinatown Ghosts** by Jim Wong-Chu, (Arsenal Pulp Press, 1986).

Eric Finney: 'Water Project', © Eric Finney. By permission of the author.

John Foster: 'Graveyard Scene', © John Foster 1991, from **Four O'clock Friday**, Oxford University Press. Included by permission of the author

Margaret Gleave: 'Washing the Sky' (first published in **Kissing the Clouds**, Driftwood Publications, 2005), by permission of the author.

Mike Jubb: 'Water Cycle', by permission of the author.

Wes Magee: 'Snagger's Pond', © Wes Magee, by permission of the author.

Lorraine Marwood: 'To Solve a Drought', first published in **Redback Mansion**, Five Islands Press, 2002, © Lorraine Marwood. By permission of the author.

Kevin McCann: 'The River', © Kevin McCann 2006. By permission of the author.

Tony Mitton,: © Tony Mitton, 2006. Originally published in **My Hat and All That** (Random House Children's Books)

Andrew Fusek Peters: 'Water-Cycle', first published in **The Moon is on the Microphone**, Sherborne Publications, 1997. 'Man, the Mad Magician', © Andrew Fusek Peters. By permission of the author.

Polly Peters: 'Girl, 13, Malawi' and 'Girl, 13, UK', © Polly Peters. By permission of the author.

Jack Prelutsky: 'Nine Mice' by Jack Prelutsky. Text copyright © Jack Prelutsky 1984. Used by permission of HarperCollins Publishers.

Nick Toczek: 'Pull the Other One', by permission of the author.

Philip Waddell: 'Pull the Other One', by permission of the author.

Colin West: 'Rodney Reid' © Colin West. Reprinted with permission of the author.

Every effort has been made to trace the copyright holders, but in some cases this has not proved possible. The publisher will be happy to rectify any such errors or omissions in future reprints and/or new editions.

Picture credits

Cover: © Myron Jay Dorf/Corbis p.6: © David Zimmerman/Corbis; p.11: Simon Borrough; p.12: © Robert Essel NYC/Corbis; p.13: © Stephen Maka/Photex/zefa/Corbis; p.14: © James L. Amos/Corbis; p.15: istockphoto; p.16: © Natalie Fobes/Corbis; p.17: © James Nazz/Corbis; p.18-19: © Gary W. Carter/Corbis; p.20-21: © Richard T. Nowitz/Corbis; p.21: © Randy Faris/Corbis; p.22: © Peter Short/istockphoto p.23: © Alex Bramwell/istockphoto; p.24: © Joe Houghton/istockphoto; p.25: © Lumenstock/Corbis; p.26: © Juergen Sack/istockphoto; p.27: © Jens Nieth/zefa/Corbis

THE ELEMENTS IN POETRY

Poems from the other books in this series

THE FLIGHT OF ICARUS

I rose on wings of wax,
Tracing angel tracks.

The sun called out my name
And I took reckless aim

Upward - the chosen one
First to kiss the Sun!

I started to perspire
In universal fire,

As if God struck a match
And somehow I could catch

Its light and hold it long…
I was wrong.

J PATRICK LEWIS

Taken from **Fire** ISBN 0 237 52885 1 (13-digit ISBN 978 0 237 52885 0)

THE GOOD EARTH

More precious than gold,
Some call it mud
But earth makes bodies
Bone and blood.
It grows the plants
Which feed us all
So, birds and beasts,
Both large and small
Come from earth
As humans do.
Earth has grown
Me and you.
More precious than gold,
Don't call it mud,
Call it bodies,
Bone and blood.

Marian Swinger

Taken from **Earth** ISBN 0 237 52887 8 (13-digit ISBN 978 0 237 52887 4)

BLUEBOTTLE

Who dips, dives,
swoops out of space,
a buzz in his wings
and sky on his face;
now caught in the light,
now gone without trace,
a sliver of glass,
never still in one place?

Who's elusive as a pickpocket,
lord of the flies;
who moves like a rocket,
bound for the skies?
Who's catapult, aeroplane,
always full-throttle?
Sky-diver, Jumping Jack,
comet,
bluebottle!

Judith Nicholls

Taken from **Air** ISBN 0 237 52888 6 (13-digit ISBN 978 0 237 52888 1)

About the anthologist

Andrew Fusek Peters, together with his wife Polly, has written and edited over 45 books for young people. Their last two verse collections were nominated for the Carnegie Medal and his poems have been recorded for the Poetry Archive (www.poetryarchive.org). His collection Mad, Bad & Dangerously Haddock features the best of his poetry for children over the last 20 years and his anthology Sheep Don't Go To School has been recommended by QCA as part of their Reading Differences scheme. Out of Order, his last anthology for the Evans Publishing Group, was highly praised.

"…an experienced and accomplished anthologist" TES

"His anthologies are always surprising and interesting. He's done it again…" Books for Keeps five star review.

Andrew is also an experienced schools' performer, quite a good juggler and mean didgeridoo player. Check him out on www.tallpoet.com.